OTHER TITLES BY THE AUTHOR

Gahan Wilson's Graveyard Manner
The Man in the Cannibal Pot
I Paint What I See
The Weird World of Gahan Wilson
Gahan Wilson's Cracked Cosmos
Gahan Wilson's Favorite Tales of Horror
And Then We'll Get Him
Nuts

Gahan Wilson's AMERICA

by
Gahan Wilson

SIMON AND SCHUSTER   NEW YORK

Copyright © 1985 by Gahan Wilson
All rights reserved
including the right of reproduction
in whole or in part in any form
Published by Simon and Schuster
A Division of Simon & Schuster, Inc.
Simon & Schuster Building
Rockefeller Center
1230 Avenue of the Americas
New York, New York, 10020
SIMON AND SCHUSTER and colophon are registered trademarks of
Simon & Schuster, Inc.
Designed by Eve Kirch
Manufactured in the United States of America

10   9   8   7   6   5   4   3   2   1

Library of Congress Cataloging in Publication Data
Wilson, Gahan.
   Gahan Wilson's America.
   1. United States—Social life and customs—
1971–   —Caricatures and cartoons.   2. American
wit and humor, Pictorial.   I. Title   II. Title:
America
E169.02.W58   1985   306'.0973   85-19672
ISBN: 0-671-55512-X

Contents

Introduction   7

1.
How It All Began   11

2.
The Wild West   17

3.
Roads and Cars   23

4.
Eating Out   33

5.
Kids   39

6.
Dating and Marriage   53

7.
Home   57

8.
Business   63

9.
Crime and the Courts   69

10.
Of Sound Bodies and Minds   73

11.
Keep Smiling   79

12.
Religion   85

13.
Electronic America   93

14.
Sports and Fitness   97

15.
Entertaining and Entertainment   103

16.
Made in Hollywood   109

17.
Urban America   117

18.
Back to Nature   125

19.
Going Abroad   131

20.
The Ultimate Escape   141

Introduction

There's no satisfactory way to explain the United States or even to describe it since it's so big it goes out of sight in all directions, and the parts in any given view reliably contradict one another. Strangers to our shores have explained bits and pieces brilliantly, but our vastness and confusion usually baffle them in the end, or at least wear them out.

Native-born citizens fare little better since any one of us must view the nation from our own particular local perspective and it has been shown many times over that, say, a Midwesterner's, Southerner's, and New Englander's separate versions of Chillicothe, not to mention their pronunciations of it, will strike a Southern Californian as hopelessly inept individually and irreconcilable as a reasonable survey. And when that Southern Californian attempts to advance his or her own supposedly more accurate version of the matter, it will draw the same healthy reaction of superficially tolerant skepticism and underlying general lack of respect as was given the others' previous accounts.

Some say this wide variety in point of view may be diminishing and that we may be blanding out like the cheeses in a supermarket. They claim that we are all striving for indistinguishability and that we may soon be as hard to tell apart as so many sitcoms. While I will grudgingly admit this does seem (I won't go further than seem) to be happening to some of our population, it is equally obvious that there is also very visibly afoot a spreading, gutsy kind of counterrevolution in which increasing numbers of Americans are striking out in an uncountable number of directions exploring, sometime successfully, sometimes not so successfully, both new—sometimes freshly invented for the purpose—and sometimes old—occasionally downright ancient—ways to blossom individually.

"Sir, the American expedition has produced conflicting reports."

So, since our naturally obstinate national ways seem to be persisting—thank heavens—any looking-over of this country, from whatever source, should be automatically viewed as partial and prejudiced by the intelligent observer, and the material in this volume is certainly no exception.

The book is also true to the national spirit in being occasionally self-contradictory, but that is as it should be since I was born and grew up in the Midwest —where you always pretend it's a good day even if you and all about you know perfectly well it's not—and then lived the bulk of my life, or have so far, in New York—where you tend to knock the good days just to show you're tough.

Also (somebody's bound to spot it so I might as well admit it right up front) there aren't any baseball cartoons in this book, and I know that is a shocker for a book about America. Anybody who is familiar with my work knows I have done baseball cartoons, quite a few of them, but when I checked over the contents of this collection just before handing it over to the publisher I couldn't find one. Then again—I did check it over in quite a hurry—maybe there is a baseball cartoon in here somewhere or other after all. Let's hope so.

"You sure this is such a good idea?"

1 How It All Began

I clearly remember being told as an innocent child that George Washington chopped down a cherry tree as a little boy and when caught red-handed at it (the pictures always showed young George with the smoking ax in his hand and the slain tree lying at his feet) he confessed, saying, "I cannot tell a lie," and that everybody from then on—including the teacher who was handing me this garbage with a totally straight face—seemed to think that made him an admirable little fellow. I also clearly remember thinking: (1) It was an insult for them to think I would swallow this junk just because I was a kid; (2) If I ever chopped down a cherry tree or even uprooted one of the scrawny little bushes growing around my apartment house nothing I could say, and certainly nothing as dense as "I cannot tell a lie," would stop all grown-ups within reach from whacking me and then barring me from Saturday movies, money for ice-cream sodas, and anything else they could think of that I wanted.

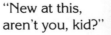
"New at this, aren't you, kid?"

I doubt nowadays if any teacher would dare try to fob off that on the children in their classrooms as they would certainly be rudely insulted by their students and perhaps even physically attacked (some things have gotten better), but I see nothing wrong in offering the fabrications assembled in this section. Anyhow, I always did suspect Ben Franklin of being up to no good.

"What do you say we give Chief Wapapatame here another of those Thanksgiving punches before talking over that little land deal?"

"Oh, very well—this court rules that the people of Salem, Massachusetts, agree to drop all charges of witchcraft against Abigail Goodey, provided the said Abigail Goodey removes her curse from the people of Salem, Massachusetts!"

"We've scouted the Delaware and it's safe for your crossing, General Washington!"

"It strikes me Ben Franklin's electrical experiments have grown quite out of hand."

"You know, it's just possible your wonderful concept of the assembly line might have larger applications, Mr. Ford."

"That is not the mood we're trying to get across out here, Parker!"

2 The Wild West

In the nineteenth century it was possible to be commemorated for advising people to "Go West," and those who took that advice helped to create the largest and most enduring of American myths. Today, no matter where they grow up geographically, most Americans spend a large part of their youth in the Wild West. My favorite part of the Wild West in Evanston, Illinois, was a vacant lot (long since built over, I am sure) which had a swell slope you could roll down, tumbling over and over and groaning horribly, after you had been shot. My first serious lessons on the West were given to me by Hopalong Cassidy and Tom Mix via extremely low-budget movies, and it was only years and years later that I realized the other kids and I spoke in the stilted, slow way we did when we played cowboys and Indians because we were conscientiously imitating terribly incompetent actors.

Everyone's agreed the real Wild West tended to be pretty awful. Most Indians, for example, had a rotten time of it. Many still do.

The cowboys were not much better off, being the underpaid, overworked servants of employers who sometimes used them cruelly.

And there were few man-to-man shoot-outs, since murderers—then as now—are a cowardly lot and uninclined to play fair.

But even before the real Wild West had faded, people began making a game of it. Of course there were numerous false starts. . . .

18

"Playing cowboy," like most games, was brought to classic form by the very rich.

It spread everywhere and kids played it for years.

With the passage of time, however, their interest shifted to other fields.

Some of those who had played cowboy remembered it, and started to revive it in a more serious, adult form.

The basic techniques were studied and perfected.

Phrases and scraps of dialogue in old movies were analyzed and learned by heart.

The props and costumes were vastly improved by an eager business community.

This time, mistakes were few and far between (although they *did* happen).

Rich people from other lands flocked to play the game.

And now, technology has insured that a day of playing cowboy is safe and thoroughly enjoyable for all.

A short nap is always recommended after the exciting activities. . . .

. . . and then the tradition is to have a comfortable dinner with one's friends.

"Remember, children—always crawl along the stripe!"

3 Roads and Cars

Of course all those comings and goings to the Far West (and the Deep South, and the Frozen North) permanently gave us all what amounts to an addiction for travel—we're probably the least geographically attached people on earth—and a deep, abiding affection for our highways. We love them all, from the long, flat Western super-routes shooting straight as arrows to the narrow New England roads meandering along their winding old ways. We clutter up their sides with distracting signs (which most of us secretly enjoy) and dream up wanderers' legends about them—about what your headlights might pick up, for instance, if you find yourself on such and such a highway, very late at night, alone.

I think, sometimes, the happiest childhood recollections of my family are of those times when we were all together in the family car going somewhere. It didn't matter where, the important thing was that we were moving away from one place, leaving it increasingly far behind, and heading off for another.

"You sure this is such a good idea?"

"You just wait!"

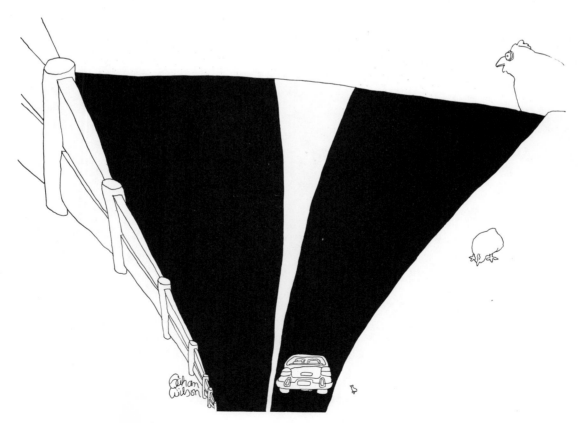

"Well, we're obviously headed in the wrong direction."

How important has the car become to us? In a legendary time long ago, there was a shortage of oil here and it looked as if we might all have to cut back seriously on our automobile travel, or be forced to travel only in dinky little cars which wouldn't be able to roar, or, impossibly, we might just have to stay put. It's nice to be nostalgic about that, and the Great Depression, and various other things you're glad aren't taking place now.

In any case, the oil shortage is over—nobody seems to be really and truly sure just where it came from or went back to—but my speculations might come in handy if it ever decides to return.

If we ever really actually do run out of oil and its useful derivatives it won't mean that we will have to change all our little ways of life; we are a clever and resourceful nation and will manage to carry on very much as we did before—we'll just do it a little slower.

As usual, the rich and powerful will be inconvenienced less than anyone else. Indeed, it's probable that they will consider this more direct domination of others an improvement.

Longer journeys will be very difficult and, in time, the interstate road system may be abandoned through lack of use. If you are born in Milwaukee, you will probably die in Milwaukee.

Trucking will continue, but the proud cruisers of yesteryear will become a fading memory. Large objects such as pianos will tend to stay where they are.

Expressways will be easily adapted to the new traffic, but the traffic itself will have to strain to keep the steady pace needed for smooth transport flow. Slower runners will be confined to back roads.

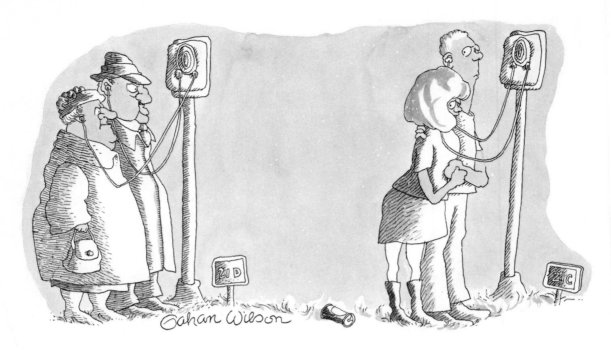

Some activities will vanish completely. Drive-in movies will try to convert to walk-in movies, but fail.

The lack of buses and subway cars will only give public transit companies new excuses for increasingly poor service and higher fares. The idea of having to walk to work may discourage muggers. Now and then someone will fall from a subway platform and be trampled by running passengers.

Motorcycleless gangs will be out of shape and fairly easy to outrun.

A heartwarming survival will be the continuation of the great American tradition of fathers and sons battling furiously, only now their endless struggle will be over who uses the family shoes.

There will, tragically, still be hit-and-run accidents. Fruitless campaigns against drunken walking will be organized. Collisions with trees and road signs will produce fewer fatalities than before.

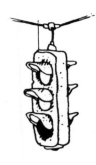

Many gas stations will survive by going into shoe service, but there will be problems in adapting to the changeover.

Drag racing will be quieter and burn less rubber.

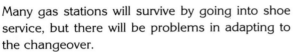

The competitive urge will continue, and shoe races will be enthusiastically attended. Now and then a souped-up sock or garter will burst into flames and give the crowd what it came for.

The wholesome virtues of the motor age will be carried on into the motorless one. Dad will have the fun of shopping for new "boots," and salesmen will encourage him to give them a testing kick as he did the tires of old.

War will be modified, perhaps for the better, as in the Tank Corps action pictured above. The return of sailpower to the Navy will produce some very pretty battles.

Emergency services will deteriorate badly since anything needed to be done quickly will not be. Ambulance patients will rarely survive their leisurely trip to the hospital. It may be, however, that we will find this enforced return to a noticeably less hectic way of life to be not without its advantages. Only time will tell.

"... Well, I couldn't *believe* I'd actually got them eating *corn,* right? But there they were, *doing* it! So I figured, what the hell! Why not try it? And I said, 'Hey —you people ever thought of having a *turkey* for dinner?' "

4 Eating Out

Native American food originated with native Americans. After that, it took a while—three centuries, in fact—for a new national cuisine to emerge. Our love of getting from one place to another in a hurry was largely what did it, along with the aforementioned roads and cars. The new food is noteworthy on two counts: It is absorbed while losing as little time as possible, and it can be relied upon to taste exactly the same in any state of the union.

"Fast food!"

"For Godsake, fellows, it was just a silly little joke!"

"Take your time, sir."

...Not that there aren't plenty of us who enjoy spending more time and money at the business of eating out. Opportunities are varied; there are those who are attracted to the novel or the exotic (especially those of us who *are* exotic), sometimes going all out for the occasion (we *have* to be the country that invented the lobster bib), and sometimes we bite off a little more than we can chew.

"I guess it's really not the right neighborhood for a sidewalk cafe."

"Captain, this Brie is totally out of control!"

"Well, I think the idea of a mime restaurant is *cute!*"

"My God, Carter—what a *stupid* place to bring L.J.!!!

"Apparently he didn't want to eat it, he wanted to play with it."

"Poor Harold always *did* have trouble with seafood."

"What have you done *now*, Willy Smith?"

5 Kids

American kids are a particularly interesting bunch, not just because of the wild variety they come in, but because our society is such a mixed bag of ethnic backgrounds and contrasting cultures that parents here are more or less forced to fake it when they bring up their children as they just don't have an agreed-on, clear-cut national code to fall back on. The result is that everybody is brought up more or less day by day, depending on what feels right at the time.

Of course all the grown-ups agree, as they have throughout history, that kids will be bad whenever they figure they can get away with it, and so, at least as far as I can remember, do the kids.

"Hi, son, I'm your first authority figure!"

In any case, no matter what area of the country you are born in, growing up is definitely not easy, as every area is packed with adults insisting that you learn by heart and obey vast amounts of information they believe is vital to your well-being. Some of this is perfectly sensible stuff and only the natural laziness and simple obstinacy of childhood prevents you from absorbing it all at the first hearing.

Take the business of not sticking your tongue out at ladies' backs: Everybody knows that's fundamentally wrong and is done only out of pure evil, and that is why it IS done.

Also, all kids are born with the sure knowledge in their bones that they should never, *ever* walk on graves . . .

(Don't) stick your tongue out at ladies' backs.

. . . and, way before harsh experience proves the terrible truth of it, there have never been any children in the entire history of our nation who have not been perfectly sure and certain that their mother should have been obeyed when she said, "Don't play in the dining room now."

(Don't) play in the dining room now.

40

But there are some things which seem irresistibly *right* to every American child even when they know they are *wrong*. Who, for example, has ever been able not to bother the dog? And has the dog ever really minded?

(Don't) bother the dog.

Has anybody ever stopped the Smith boy from eating weird stuff? No, because then they would never have found out the interesting thing that happened when he did.

And the same simple curiosity has goaded every one of us of any intelligence to eat dog food . . .

(Don't) let the Smith boy eat weird stuff.

(Don't) eat dog food.

. . . and far, far too much of various other things in order to see whether or not we would get violently ill and possibly even die.

(Don't) eat until you die.

Of course it has to be admitted that a number of naughty things are done because of simple perversity. There is no child, of any state in this union, who has not gone all floppy when his mother tried to dress him . . .

(Don't) go all floppy when people try to dress you.

. . . or who has not deliberately stepped off a path in the park . . .

(Don't) step off the path.

. . . or who has not tried to see how badly they could damage themselves with their favorite sport . . .

(Don't) skip rope until you die.

. . . but few of us have been evil enough to actually NOT watch our baby brother on the beach . . .

(Don't) forget to watch your little brother.

... or dared sit there in the dark and watch TV all day long in order to see whether we really would get moldy ...

(Don't) watch TV in the dark all day long.

... and it is almost scientifically certain that none of us, not one, was ever able to entirely convince ourself that there really was nothing under the bed.

(Don't) believe there is something under your bed.

This last one brings us to a whole series of important childhood beliefs which many adults have forgotten, or at least pretend to have forgotten. These beliefs are firmly held this very minute by children growing up in Florida and all the way over to Alaska. Some do not figure in their day-to-day lives, being in the category of child legends which hopefully will never actually be personally experienced . . .

"Wrong door!"

. . . but the other beliefs, the majority of them, are always hovering at the edges of any kid's mind just as surely as adult beliefs such as "you should cross only with the green light."

These beliefs are obscure and benighted, having been developed entirely within the children's own society, which is secret and hidden from that of the adult one around them and is as strange and alien to it as any found practiced by surviving Stone Age tribes come across in isolated Pacific islands or discovered tucked away in some dark bend of the Amazon. Indeed, there is probably no group of humans living on this earth more shuddersomely superstitious, or more grotesquely misinformed, than the ordinary children we see pottering about daily at our knee level.

Constantly forced to obey the imcomprehensible rules of a society they cannot even dimly begin to understand, menaced by awesome diseases and fearsome technological poisons, endlessly presented with unanswerable questions, these tiny creatures—in a brave, if faltering, attempt to cope with and explain to themselves their basically alien environment—have created a rich trove of hopelessly inept cautionary beliefs of which the following selection represents only the most superficial skimming.

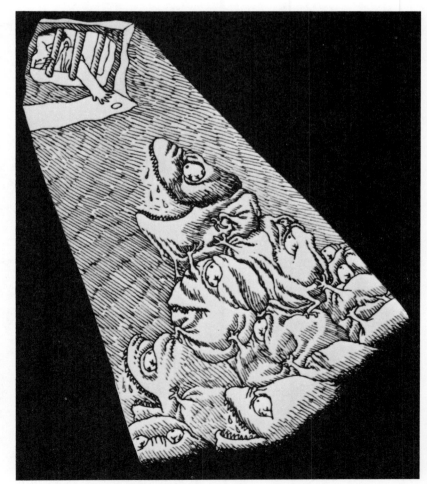

Storm Drain Biters

If a coin or a ball or a marble rolls into the opening of a storm drain, the wise child will try to claw it out with a stick or just leave it alone, as there are things down there which very much enjoy *biting off fingers.*

Swinging Over the Bar

Swinging over the bar is to be avoided at all costs for it will turn the swinger inside out.

Counting Every Board

Compulsion is an important aspect of children's beliefs. Whose life has not been severely bent because they failed or did not fail to accept some dare or cross or not cross a line someone has drawn? Here is a typically suicidal self-imposed challenge—the child has vowed he will touch each and every board, *and count it,* on the way home. If he does not do this, he knows that he will be eaten.

Making a Face

If you make a face and are slapped on the back unexpectedly while doing it, the face will stay that way for the rest of your life. If you stick your tongue too far out, it will stay like that for the rest of your life, and if you cross your eyes wrong, they will stick crossed for the whole rest of your life.

Step on a Crack and Break Your Mother's Back

Very few children actually believe this, but probably there is not one child who has not tried it, just to see.

The Awful Stuff in the Center of a Golf Ball

If you cut down into the center of a golf ball, there is this horrible acid that destroys everything. Somebody once told me they had done it but I saw they weren't horribly burned so I knew they were lying. I got down as far as where it gets rubbery once.

Water Fountain Germs

Children know there are germs on water fountains, but are vague on what germs are. They know they are nasty and slimy things. Probably they jump.

Kissing Grandma

If you kiss grandma your lips will get all wrinkled up like hers as it is catching, but of course there is no way to avoid kissing grandma.

Getting Cramps from Eating

If you eat anything, even half a hot dog, and you go into the water less than a half hour later, you will get terrible cramps. If you are swimming, you will sink like a stone.

The Toilet Monster

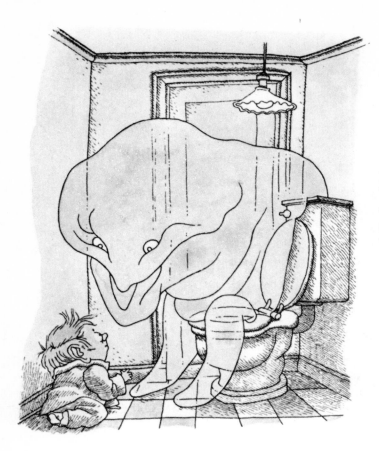

I never knew about this when I was a child, thank God. There's this thing that lives in the toilet, and *likes* it, and when you go late at night and flush the toilet it *wakes the thing up,* so you better hurry getting out of there. This kid was too slow.

The Exploding Boy

If you block a sneeze wrong, you can burst your eardrums. If you block a burp wrong, you can burst your throat. If you block a fart wrong, you can burst your asshole. If you do all of these at once, this is what happens.

Eating Milk and Cherries Together is Poison

This boy told his parents that eating milk and cherries together would kill him, but they wouldn't believe him and they made him do it and now they are sorry.

Mr. Knudson, the Super, Sets Traps in the Basement

Building superintendents have all kinds of reasons to want to *get* children, good reasons, and so children understand that they will probably have what they deserve if they are not very careful. It's a good idea to be especially wary around the furnace.

Jagging Off

If you jag off you will become very ill and pale and have blue sacs under your eyes. Also hair will sprout on the palm of the hand you jag off with. Also you may go crazy. Now that you are jagging off it is time you left strange beliefs of children behind and took up those of adolescents. They are fun too.

Getting Warts from a Toad

Of course if you touch a toad you will get warts from it and probably swell up and turn green too.

Lead Pencil Poisoning

If you poke the point of a lead pencil into your skin, you will get lead poisoning and die horribly. There is absolutely nothing that can be done to save you.

"I'm so glad you could meet my folks!"

6 Dating and Marriage

"Who's that?"

Love is very popular here, as it seems to be in all countries, but I have often wondered if we are clumsier about it than most others. I wondered about this particularly when I was dating, particularly in school. I think things are better now. For example, I don't think they make you go to dance classes, which make you hate dancing for the rest of your life, anymore, and by and large the kids seem to wear less embarrassing clothes. I saw a high school prom recently, though, and it looked as if they are just as agonizing and as heartbreaking today as they were back in the good old days. I certainly wished the kids well.

Of course dating leads to other things, very often to marriage, and marriage very often leads to divorce, but that sometimes almost seems a waste of time as, more often than not, that only leads to another marriage. It's a free country.

"I can't wait till I see Daddy's face when he gets a look at you!"

"You're always trying too hard, Eddie!"

"You're not having much fun, are you? I like that in a man."

"Gee, Amelia, I'm really very sorry you won't be able to make it here tonight."

"As my late husband, here, used to say. . . ."

"I want to leave you, Edna. Where do I go?"

7 Home

Even if we are a migrating people (we were nomads to start with or we wouldn't be here in the first place), most of us—from a street person fumbling together a little doorway nest out of corrugated boxes to a railroad baron adding another hotel-sized wing to his Bar Harbor mansion—at least attempt to put together some version of a home, even if we're not sure we'll stay put.

Once we've installed ourselves in our home we are free to pursue our hobbies and putterings-around, and we very often install pets, in turn, so that they may pursue their own hobbies and putterings-around, and the whole thing helps to pass the time very nicely.

"My husband, of course, will want a den."

"I think they're going to take it!"

"Here comes Howard, now!"

"I like this view. It lets you alone."

"I tell you, Agnes, I just *dread* the Fourth!"

"Here he comes with his goddamned yearly contract!"

"Forgot to add water again, didn't you?"

"Good morning, Mr. Tremont."
"Good morning, Mr. Tremont."
"Good morning, Mr. Tremont."
"Good morning, Mr. Tremont."
"Good morning, R. T."
"Good morning, R. T."
"Morning, R. T."
"How's it going, Bob?"

8 Business

The fact is that without business a lot of us wouldn't have any idea what to do with ourselves during weekdays, and weekends can be gotten through only if we've had the foresight to take something home from the office. Of course we all staunchly pretend we're looking forward to retirement, but there are very few of us who are not secretly glad we haven't gotten there yet.

The result of all this is that people spend a lot more time at business than they'd intended to at the start and find it spreading out over large parts of their lives which were not supposed to be business at all. Lunch, for instance, was doubtless initially designed as a respite from business, but it has become, for an increasing number of executives, the toughest and most demanding part of their working day (though it may soon take a back seat to the power breakfast, which is the new meal in town).

Of course business has been affected by progress, which is to say that working people on all levels now find themselves increasingly in competition with the computers and other machinery initially designed to serve them. But that is the way things go in a free market.

"You're not going to get anywhere with me, Barker, until you realize I'm lovable."

"Tell him I'm still busy and put him on hold again with that horrible music!"

"Didn't go for it, eh?"

64

"I will have the senior-executive businessman's lunch, and Harper, here, will have the junior-executive businessman's lunch."

"I'd hate to think that the idea I can buy and sell you would get in the way of our friendship, Harry."

"I'm glad you asked me that question."

"May I make a suggestion?"

"What's that pretty little pink one mean?"

"I don't suppose I'm the first person to point out the strong resemblance between you and your father."

"It's just that sort of thing which has me worrying about R. H.!"

"I think it's his beeper!"

"... Well, my goodness—*yes*... Now I, really come to think of it... I guess, in a crazy, funny kind of way, we're *all* sort of guilty!"

9 **Crime and the Courts**

Just a few steps away from business we come to crime, which employs the same essential techniques but carries them just a little too far. Very often the difference between a legitimate enterprise and an illegal one is merely a question of excess. If you force someone to hand something over to you by threatening to destroy them financially, that is business, but if you menace their skull with a club you have lapsed over into bad taste and crime. That is why people who are too dense to understand the nuance which separates the two are liable to behave with extreme righteous indignation when caught and brought to trial. Such trials take place in courts—which thanks to cable TV are becoming a thriving part of America's entertainment industry.

In any case, I am all for law and order. I only wish they worked better.

". . . If I might have your Honor's undivided attention?"

"I'm very touched, fellows."

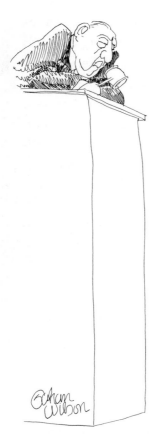

"It is the opinion of this court you are not a very funny stand-up comic."

"...Are you really, *really* sorry?"

"You'd think over the years one or two of them would catch on."

"Now these pills you just took will have some visual side-effects."

10 Of Sound Bodies and Minds

Getting sick in America is particularly terrifying, not so much because of the illnesses themselves (though we do seem to have a peculiar talent for developing, or at least popularizing, new diseases), but because the doctors here are so inventive when it comes to putting things into us, or taking them out of us, or just plain diagnosing us. It seems we are continually in danger of being seriously damaged even if it does finally turn out that we were actually in fine shape all the time.

Until the brain transplant is perfected, our minds will probably continue to be serviced by one of our more complex medical industries, psychiatry, though it presently contains so many contrasting, if not downright antagonistic, disciplines to choose from that many would-be patients never get past that first stage.

"I just *hate* it when patients get uppity!"

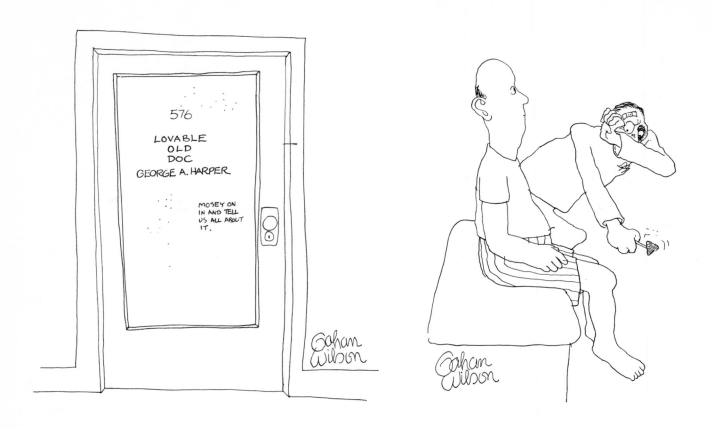

"It's a lot more fun this way, isn't it?"

"His heart is broken."

"You're not much on small talk, are you?"

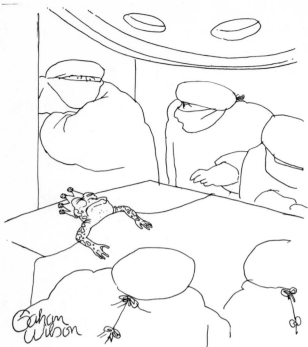

"OK, he's ready—bring in the beautiful maid!"

"I'd like to help you but, frankly, I'm intimidated."

"We may have made a significant breakthrough today, Dr. Jekyll."

"We must find out what is driving you from one incompetent psychiatrist to another!"

"It's what we call an 'evil sending'!"

"No, really, doctor—the resemblance is quite extraordinary!"

11 **Keep Smiling**

Psychiatry (or its failures) leads us to what may be one of the most depressing things ever thought of, which is: the little round face with the great big smile—perhaps the single most embarrassing invention in American history.

You know the little smiling face, don't you? Of course you do. You've seen it printed on scratchy napkins in bad restaurants, you've seen it on cheap labels stuck to tacky toys, you've observed it in one way or another associated with all sorts of third-rate things which the people trying to foist them on you *know* in their heart of hearts are mediocre.

The little face is a bully that insists you smile even if you don't mean it at all, even if your smile will be as big a fake as the product bearing the little face. It represents phony fun, and there are few things drearier than phony fun. The worst, most unforgivable aspect of the smile on the round face is that it insults *real* smiles, which are the most valuable things we have.

Were you unfortunate enough to have a smiling-face mobile hanging over your crib? Did you wonder why it made you snivel? Did it make you feel guilty because you weren't smiling back? Of course it did.

Remember the first time a grown-up told you to go outside and have some phony fun? You couldn't quite figure out what was wrong because you were too young and innocent and trusting to know he was a simp and had no idea what fun was and never would, but that's why when you went out and tried to follow his advice it didn't work. It wasn't your fault at all. Now you know.

How about your first birthday party? Remember how everybody insisted you have fun and got mad when you couldn't? Of course you figured you were to blame . . .

. . . and the memory of it has spoiled countless parties for you since.

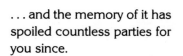

You can't forget the doctor clown at the circus even yet, can you? Everybody else seemed to think he was lots of fun.

Remember when the whole family had to have fun, and never admit afterward they hadn't or your parents would throw a fit?

At summer camp you realized it wasn't just a domestic problem; anyone would do anything to anyone else anywhere, to try and have a little fun.

As you grew older you discovered increasingly horrible ways to have fun. Along with everybody else.

Remember the fun you had with your first whore?

Fun really came into its own on the holidays! It was an official duty! You had to have fun in order to keep on making a living. But not too much.

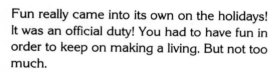

New Year's Eve was particularly effective because it underlined your total failure to have fun for the last twelve months.

Let's not even discuss your trip abroad and how you're still lying to everyone about how much fun you had.

Of course retirement is supposed to be the high fun point of everybodys' career. If you're lucky, you may miss it.

And let's all pray that whoever invented the smiling face didn't go to heaven!

"Well, Rev. Parker, all I can say is that was a pretty convincing demonstration."

12 **Religion**

If neither medicine nor psychiatry work, as does happen, there is always religion. One of the nicest things about America is that it does grant official freedom to its citizens to choose any religion they want, and of course that means that many of us citizens tend to overdo it, and if we don't like what's already available, we'll often work out something brand new all on our own.

There does tend to be a rough geographic clumping of religious tendencies, but every area offers a generous range of choices. California may lead all other states in Space Age religions, but it also has Forest Lawn, and the generally conservative Bible Belt is peppered with small groups following the most esoteric persuasions, including institutions devoted to electronically stimulated astral travel.

"Of course none of that stuff counts for *you,* Mr. Carter!"

It was just this wide-ranging field of possibilities that got me started to fantasizing what might happen if the whole thing got into the wrong hands. What if some particularly tasteless entrepreneur (we do have them) decided to get into religion on a purely commercial basis? We might all be unfortunate enough to end up with:

... That's right, Mr. and Mrs. Leisure America, HOLYLAND℠ is an *entirely new concept* in devotional recreation! *Not* an amusement park, *not* a shrine, *not* another fly-by-night "pilgrim trap," HOLYLAND℠ is more than just a fun-filled weekend ... it's a *deeply moving religious experience!* Yes! Not only is HOLYLAND℠ an exciting spiritual "happening" for adults, it's also a wonderful way to let our cherished Judeo-Christian tradition of fair play and sound business practices seep painlessly into the hearts of your little ones.

Start your day at the historic "Patriarch Pavilion" (*above*), this month's show-stopping ceremony guest-hosted by Mr. George Jessel and your choice of Lassie, Flipper, Snoopy, or E.T., each appearing for one performance, and one performance only.

Then it will be getting on toward lunchtime, so be sure to follow one of HOLYLAND's™ friendly "prophets" to the Last Supper Snak Bar, where you can choose from a fulsome menu of authentic biblical treats including Pope Tarts, Manna Splits, non-fatted Calfburgers, and sizzling St. Joan-Kebabs.

Tummy (and spirit) full? Hungry now for some challenging yet inexpensive tests of mettle? Make a pilgrimage to HOLYLAND's™ exciting "Ordeals O' Skill" boardwalk. There are so many trials to choose from, it's hard to know what to undergo first, but we're betting that high on your list will be the Salem Duck-O-Rama! Strap little Johnny down in the brightly painted ducking stool, and *splash!* he goes into the water for as long as he can stand it (or maybe just a wee bit more)! Then it's off to the HOLYLAND™ "Cast the First Stone" booth, where a quarter buys three hefty chances to "stone" the "painted woman" to "death." Of course the kids will want Dad to be a "big man" and take a turn at the "Holy Martyr Rack," and if he isn't a big man already, he certainly will be afterward.

Having fun? Sure you are! But what about the "faithful" back home? You'll be wanting to load up on postcards and souvenirs at HOLYLAND's™ Ye Olde Relick Shoppe, where there is a multitude of earthly delights to be purchased, ranging from thirty real pieces of silver embedded in a clear Lucite block to a lovely Crown o' Thorns Easter wreath to pep up your door or refrigerator for years to come. A teen in the ramily? Even the "grooviest" hepcat will "dig" the Relick Shoppe's wide assortment of "way out" Blasphemy Buttons with naughty sayings like "Christ Was a Jew" and "God Spelled Backwards Is Dog."

Say, and don't forget to have every member of the family pick up his or her crosses at the little shop on "Golgotha Way," each one appropriately scaled and weighted. Imagine what an exciting stir the kids will make when they show up dragging these reminders of their happy stay at HOLY-LAND™ into their classrooms!

Hold on there! you may be saying to yourself, Patriarch Pavilions, Ordeal O' Skill, and Blasphemy Buttons are fine and dandy, but what about the rides? Well, this small brochure cannot begin to describe the thrills and chills awaiting you at HOLYLAND™! You and your family will be "transported" with your first ride on the welt-raising Taste-the-Whip, the dizzying Catherine Wheel, and the flying Pente-Coaster!

89

Well, Mom and Dad, it's getting on toward the eleventh hour and time to call it another miraculous day at HOLYLAND™. Just enough time to take a respectful gander at the Robot Jesus as he automatically bestows upon the happy throngs a benediction in his own personal words, then gives a special blessing for the day, the correct time, and road conditions for the long drive home.

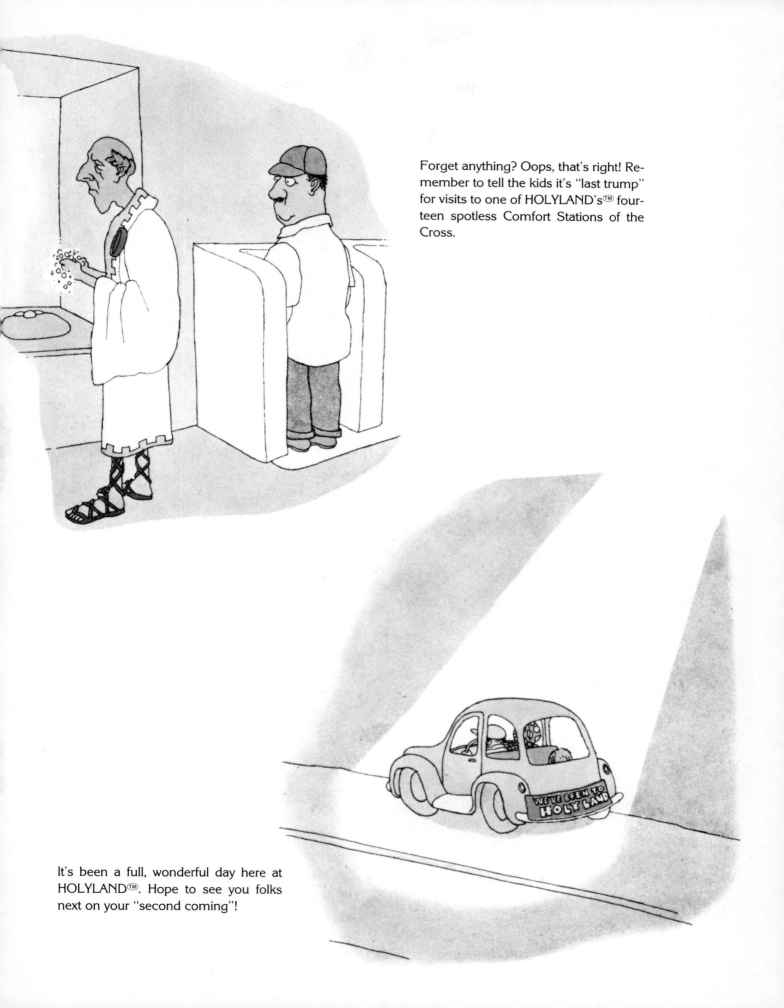

Forget anything? Oops, that's right! Remember to tell the kids it's "last trump" for visits to one of HOLYLAND's™ fourteen spotless Comfort Stations of the Cross.

It's been a full, wonderful day here at HOLYLAND™. Hope to see you folks next on your "second coming"!

13 Electronic America

Our increasingly electronic way of life is by no means exclusively American, but it is, nonetheless, the biggest obvious change that's hit us in recent times. The increasingly small size of its apparatus and the scale of its entertainment suggest that it may all be part of an unconscious preparation for space travel, but it's far too early to make any detailed guesses as to where it will all lead us. Doubtless some place totally unexpected.

"It was a very naughty TV set!"

"Mommy! Mommy! Daddy lost!"

"Would you care to try it out on the store's specimen sidewalk, Sir?"

"Here's an interesting item about a reported increase in mice. . . ."

"From now on the news will be brought to you by animated duck!"

"... And remember—it isn't whether you win or lose; it's how you play the game!"

14 Sports and Fitness

When I was growing up, sports for kids was a relatively crude business. You made do with a vacant lot or a combination of sidewalks and streets and sort of bent the game you were playing around this improvised field. Grown-ups passed by and sometimes one or two of them would stop and watch, but by and large they left us alone to play whatever we were playing by ourselves.

That's all over and has been all over for a long time now. The grown-ups invented Little Leagues and have been industriously developing them, and maybe I've got it wrong but it looks suspiciously like they've taken the game entirely away from the kids—even if it is the kids who are actually playing it— the way some fathers end up running the train set they bought their boy for Christmas.

Professional sports have gotten so tough both on the field and off that they're almost too grim for an idle pastime, and amateurs are pursuing exercise and other private sports with such fearsome dedication that it may be time someone invented a new sport which we wouldn't take so seriously and could just watch for the heck of it. At least for a while.

"Sorry, Carter, I had my mind on something else. I didn't mean to beat you that badly."

"Why can't you get one of those stationary bicycles like everyone else?"

"For God's sake, Phil—*cut the line!!!*"

More of us Americans exercise regularly today than ever before, and those of us who are surprised to find ourselves practicing it regularly have noticed little quirks concerned with its various techniques which deserve being passed on to fellow citizens considering taking up the art.

During the early days of the exercise boom wealthy people hired others to do their calesthenics for them. Time and experience eventually demonstrated that this practice seriously reduced the benefits of their body-building campaigns.

The key word in isometrics is *balance*. Make sure that every part of your body shares equally in the fun and problems will be avoided.

One should always proceed cautiously in yoga as mistakes have a way of hanging on.

When jogging watch your step as loosened internal organs have an undeniable tendency to slip into the lower limbs.

Of course it's always a good idea to make sure your equipment is installed properly.

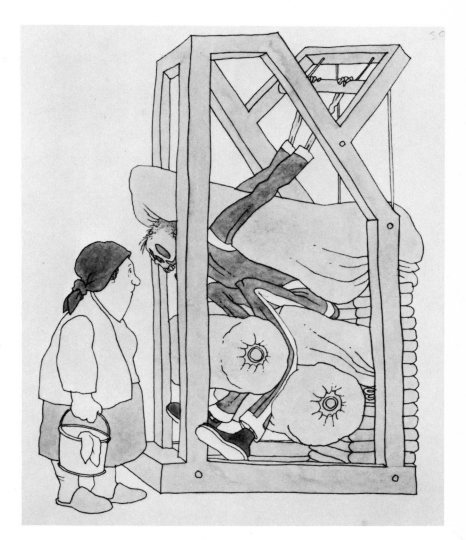

Finally, it's a good, commonsense rule never to increase the weight load of any exercise machine when you are working out by yourself.

"God, Renny, it's the ultimate disco effect!"

15 Entertaining and Entertainment

Entertaining is a nice way to pass the time. The cocktail party seems to be the basic form (though there seem to be fewer cocktails present than there used to be), but there are plenty of ingenious variations possible (including ways to entertain oneself).

Being entertained is certainly easier, and there are entertainments for all tastes: from stand-up comics to music to theater, or, on the more social side, a visit to one's club or disco.

"Bankers are real, too, you know."

"You're a contemporary novelist? Say—
I'm a contemporary novelist, myself!"

"More ice cream, anyone?"

"Have you been mean to Mr. Chair?"

". . . But, seriously . . ."

"I would like to play for you now a song of my people."

"Well, I suppose we've got to see it."

"I should hope so!"

"I guess this really *is* his farewell performance!"

"You don't turn out people like us in just a couple of generations."

"Your usual evening belt, sir?"

"The only thing I regret, really, is the club tie."

"This is the part I like best—tucking them in for the night!"

"I understand the special effects are pretty realistic!"

16 Made in Hollywood

One of the most American entertainment forms of all is, of course, the movies. Hollywood itself is a tiny but very complex place composed of odd professionals (talent agents, for example) and more swimming pools than people. But despite its smallness, Hollywood has tremendous influence on us. Most of the insides of American heads are in large part made up of what they see at the movies, and that is why everybody's personality is—aside from a few minor trimmings they've picked up from their parents and loved ones (and those very rare bits which have stuck to them from their official education)—almost entirely manufactured in Hollywood.

"What can I say? You're my kind of talent!"

An essential, if not very smart, part of most people's growing up is deciding how one should smoke a cigarette. The bulk of the great Hollywood smokers are dead, for pretty good medical reasons, but examples of their training remain long after they are gone. Erich von Stroheim, a villain of the twenties and thirties and the butler in *Sunset Boulevard,* developed a smoking technique of incredible complexity, which against all odds is still practiced by those oldsters who have managed to survive the damage it has done them. . . .

...And though Charles Boyer may no longer be with us his French inhale, wherein the smoke is sucked from the mouth through the nostrils, is studiously learned by the youngest practicing smokers, as is the Humphrey Bogart lip hold, wherein an entire cigarette is smoked without the smoker once removing it from his mouth or blinking his eyes. (Squinting is perfectly all right; in fact it adds to the effect.)

The process of assimilating the movie greats into our flesh and blood is begun very early, although the first attempts, such as the Frankenstein monster walk, the Bela Lugosi leer, and the Lon Chaney, Jr., werewolf howl, may eventually have to be abandoned for social reasons.

Sometimes we are influenced by passing fads. The pets of this country once subjected their masters to many unwanted and unasked-for rescues because of the Lassie films. . . .

. . . And the James Dean image, though still easily picked out in a crowd, no longer inspires thousands of identical rebels.

Even the Marilyn Monroe influence, sadly, seems to be fading.

There are dangers in attempting to incorporate one's film idols into one's daily life. Musical comedies can be particularly risky. Adopting the Gene Kelly image can lead to arrest. . . .

. . . And break dancing is definitely not for the elderly affluent.

Also, certain more fantastic themes should be adopted only by the very mentally healthy. An E.T. syndrome may be charming in a child . . .

. . . but it should be dropped somewhere along the road to adulthood.

The positive aspects of "living Hollywood" far outweigh the drawbacks, however. It is wonderful to live in a world which can be based in one's mind on Alfred Hitchcock . . .

. . . or, in another mood, a religious epic of Cecil B. DeMille.

You can be a W. C. Fields or a
George C. Scott drunk, as you
will . . .

. . . and since it's a free country it's
entirely up to you whether you become Woody Allen or Arnold
Schwarzenegger.

"Face it, Edwin—it isn't that we've all turned into teddy bears, it's that you've gone crazy!"

116

17 Urban America

We are, and always have been, very much on one side or the other of whether big cities are wonderful centers of culture or cesspools—almost nobody's willing to take middle ground. Whatever you think of big cities, if you are a visitor it is probably wise to approach one with a certain amount of wariness. Nobody denies that cities are large and complicated, and that their habitants live under a good deal of stress.

"But there I go, talking to myself again!"

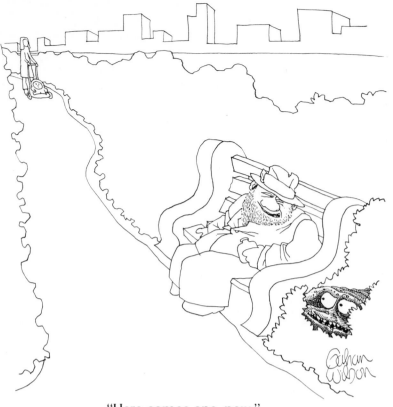

"Here comes one, now."

New York, probably more than any other major city, is a magnet for business.

It also has probably had more legends attached to it by total strangers than any other big city, and if you buy the rumors about the town that often cause would-be visitors needless nervousness and worry, your visions would probably be along the following lines. . . .

One typically misleading story is that the snakes and alligators living in the city's sewers are dangerous; nothing could be further from the truth. They are entirely harmless, and their unfailingly affectionate greetings to strangers and locals alike constitute one of the most heartwarming features of a stroll through the city's streets.

Do be careful of the trees of the Upper East Side, however. Wary New Yorkers have always carefully fenced them in, and with good reason!

One feature of the town that has not been exaggerated by legend is its potholes. . . .

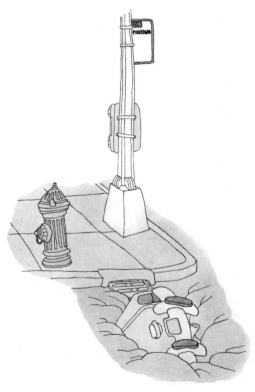

... And newcomers will be well advised to exercise reasonable caution in dealing with its sophisticated businesspeople.

Public transport is nowhere near as bad as the more sensational news media make it out to be, but the graffiti artists are always on the lookout for fresh, unmarked surfaces ...

... And it is a good idea whenever possible to avoid rush hours. ...

. . . But anything is better than the city's deadly taxis.

Food is something of a problem. The street vendors should be avoided unless one's taste is entirely urban. . . .

. . . Exotic restaurants are notorious for amusing themselves by serving out-of-towners digusting food on purpose. . . .

...And a number of fancy restaurants enjoy handing customers menus printed in no known language.

Do not stare at fashionable displays in the windows of the more exclusive department stores as you will not only seem to turn short and fat; you will actually do so.

You may have read in the newspapers that falling objects invariably maim or kill visitors from out of town. Be advised.

Central Park should, of course, be avoided. If you do have to enter it, always keep a sharp eye on the many pigeons and squirrels lurking on its lawns and walks. . . .

. . . But understand you do not have to enter it to be mugged.

And always watch out for bag ladies.

18 Back to Nature

Especially for urban Americans, it's important from time to time "to get away from it all." Of course some rural Americans already *are* away from it all, while others need only look up at our "spacious skies" for quick escapes. But to really get away, there is nature. We have a lot of nature in America, probably more of it than anything else (except sky, which come to think of it I guess has to be considered part of nature). Except in the East, there are many so-called wide-open spaces, even wilderness, and here the sophisticated vacationer can find both inspiration and adventure. But there are risks too. Our hinterlands have some hair-raising local legends, and it is possible to get stranded in places with strange customs.

"You do this sort of thing often?"

"How's things over your way?"

". . . See? And that's his nose . . . and, curling underneath, there's his mouth!"

"You don't see the night sky like this in the city!"

"It's times like these you find out if you're basically optimistic or not."

"That's a cloud, too. They're all clouds."

"Hard to believe all this was formed by natural erosion!"

"Just do me one favor, will you? Don't tell me what it reminds you of."

"Offhand, I'd say its diet goes a long way toward explaining the lack of reported sightings."

". . . And I think this here is little Norma Jean."

"Yep, I guess the full moon takes some gettin' used to if you weren't brought up hereabouts."

19 Going Abroad

Probably the most effective method for any one of us to get away from it all is to leave the whole country. Of course while it will give you a total change of pace and all sorts of interesting new experiences and many rich, fulfilling contacts with people from diverse cultures, it is also really asking for it!

Things probably won't be anywhere near as bad as the following cautionary essay might suggest, but it is always best to expect the worst, as they say, and that way anything less awful will be a happy surprise. At least that's what they used to say around where I grew up, and I can tell you it was pretty depressing.

"Tourist class and proud of it!"

In preparation for his trip, the traveler studies his phrase book, and sentences such as "I have been clubbed and am bleeding profusely" and "Please send someone to my room as I am trapped and it is aflame" set him to thinking on what he knows will happen.

I think those people are lepers.
Chznashk dwak ekaki bor shlek.
Sooz-nah-sak twah ah-gah-si buh slah-eek.

First, of course, the stevedores will abuse and defile his luggage.

The passage will set records for foul weather, the man in the upper berth will die after a terrible coughing fit, and the traveler will have difficulty discouraging the man in the lower berth, who will fancy him.

The customs officer will point out that the picture in the traveler's passport does not resemble him in the least.

He will find the country's money incomprehensible and be unable to fit it into his wallet.

The taxi will take him on a lengthy, roundabout route through strange parts of town.

The deskman at his hotel will suspect him of things.

People will spy on him.

The bathroom will be full of strange devices.

His voltage adapter will not work and his razor will be destroyed.

He will order the national dish, *Lakle Bes Cherzdny,* and find it to be rats in white cream sauce.

He will try a local medicine to counter the effects of the *Lakle* and will regret it.

The next morning he will take a short-cut and become lost in a dangerous neighborhood.

A whore will attach herself to him for blocks and then shriek curses at him.

A guide will give him misinformation about a tomb, insult his shoes, and insist on an exorbitant fee.

He will inadvertently go into the ladies' room.

He will rent a car, fail to work the gears properly, and be heavily fined.

The maps and road signs will confuse him.

When his car breaks down he will try to telephone the rental agency, but give up.

In asking directions to the railway station, he will unaccountably infuriate passersby.

Whereas his fellow passengers in the train compartment will find his appearance hilarious.

On the way to the airport a small boy will offer to carry his suitcase and steal it.

Just before leaving, he will buy his sister's youngest daughter a souvenir doll, unaware that it will make obscene gestures when wound.

He will discover the economy flight his travel agent arranged was a serious error and that instead of returning home, his trip has barely started.

"Limited nuclear war, sir, is where people like you and me survive."

20 The Ultimate Escape

Of course some of our military have a plan for getting away from it all which would be hard to beat for effectiveness. . . .

"So I guess that's it for Idaho, too, folks!"

"Way to go—hey, Harry?!"

"I think it means we'd better find some shade!"

...But let's hope we settle for something a little less extreme.

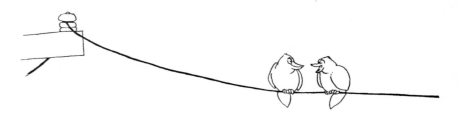

"Well, it certainly is nice to be back in West Palm Beach."

About the Author

Gahan Wilson has published seven or nine other books for adults (depending on one's distinctions of children's and adult literature). His cartoons appear regularly in *Playboy, The New Yorker, Paris Match, Punch,* and *The National Lampoon.* His qualifications to write about America include a Midwestern childhood and descent from such authentic folk heroes as P. T. Barnum and William Jennings Bryan.